DONKEY

Sandie Lee Books

Donkeys

The donkey is known by many different names. It is a member of the Equus asinus family. Its correct name is an Ass, but it is more commonly called, a donkey. In Spanish, wild donkeys are called, a Burro. A Mule is a cross between a male donkey and a female horse. A male donkey is called, a Jack and a female donkey is called, a Jenny. However, no matter what we call it, the donkey is a very cool animal. Let's explore the world of the donkey to discover more fascinating facts.

Where in the World?

Did you know domesticated (tame) donkeys can be found all over the world? The donkeys we see on farms were all descended from the African species. Wild donkeys are still found in Australia, Tibet, Nepal, Asia, the Middle East and in parts of the United States. This animal in the wild will live on desert plains and grasslands

The Body of a Donkey

Did you know the donkey is similar to a horse in its body structure? The donkey has a compact body and long slender legs. Depending on the species, it can stand from 2.9 feet to 4.9 feet at the shoulder. It has a big head and long ears. The donkey can weigh up to 570 pounds.

The Donkey's Senses

Did you know the donkey has a sweet tooth? Donkeys love the taste of sweet things. They will eat fruit and even crack open walnuts. The sense of hearing in a donkey is well-tuned. It can move its ears to pick up different sounds. Although, its sight is not great, it can still see all the major colors.

What a Donkey Eats

Did you know this animal grazes on grass? In the wild, donkeys can survive on little water and food. They will search out grass and other plants to eat. Tame donkeys are fed hay, straw and special cubes made from fiber. However, the ragwort plant is highly toxic to a donkey and should be avoided.

The Donkey's Jobs

Did you know the donkey makes a good guard animal? When a donkey has bonded with a herd of goats or sheep, it will protect them. When a donkey hears a noise it will alert the herd by a loud call. The donkey has also been used to pull wagons and to carry heavy loads on its back.

The Donkey as Prey

Did you know wild donkeys are hunted? Depending on the species of wild donkey, it can be hunted by land predators such as large cats. Man is also hunting the donkey for sport and for its meat. In the African and Chinese culture, other parts of the donkey are used in their medicines.

Donkey Talk

Did you know the donkey can make sounds? We all know donkey's can say hee-haw. This is known as braying. Some donkey's can also whinny. It will sound like whinee........ ending in an "aw ah aw." The donkey likes routine and will let their owners know when they are hungry or want to be let out of the barn.

Mom Donkey

Did you know a mother donkey can have young at 2 years-old? The mother donkey can carry her young from 11.5 to 14 months. She will give birth to one foal, as twins are extremely rare. She will nurse her foal milk for about 4 to 5 months.

Baby Donkey

Did you know the baby donkey can stand shortly after birth? Foals can stand, walk and run the first day they are born. When the foal reaches one year of age, it will be independent of its mother. It will grow for another year or two, filling out and developing.

Donkey Sleep

Did you know like horses, donkeys can sleep standing up? The donkey can fall asleep standing up because of a special joint in its legs. This joint locks to keep the donkey upright. If a donkey feels very safe, it may lie down to take a nap or to sleep at night.

Life of a Donkey

Did you know donkeys need to have other animals with it? Donkeys are very social and will become sad and even sick when left alone. A donkey on a farm can live to be from 25 to 40 years-old. Wild donkeys live in herds and sometimes only live to be around 10 years-old.

Mammoth Donkey

This species of donkey is the largest of them all. It can grow to be 4.9 feet at the shoulder. Its fur can be black, brown or reddish in color. Like all donkeys, it has long ears and slender legs. This donkey has been domesticated and is kept on farms and as pets.

Miniature Mediterranean

This species of donkey is very small. It can measure from 2.5 feet to 2.8 feet at the shoulder. It is a loving and kind beast. This donkey is very social and needs to be with other animals. It is quite smart and makes a wonderful pet.

Poitou Donkey

This donkey is native to France. It is a large breed that stands close to 5 feet at the shoulder. This donkey's coat is extremely long. If left uncut, it will grow in long soft cords. This is called, cadanette. Its coat is always dark brown or black in color. Its underbelly is white and it will have rings around its eyes and white on its nose.

Quiz

Question 1: What is the Spanish word for Donkey?

Answer 1: Burro

Question 2: What do donkey's love to eat?

Answer 2: Sweet things

Question 3: What special job can the donkey perform?

Answer 3: It can guard other animals or a farm

Question 4: What can a baby donkey do shortly after it is born?

Answer 4: It can stand, walk and run

Question 5: What is the biggest donkey breed called?

Answer 5: The mammoth donkey

Thank you for checking out another addition from Sandie Lee Books! Make sure to check out Amazon.com for many other great titles.

www.ingramcontent.com/pod-product-compliance
Lightning Source LLC
Chambersburg PA
CBHW050801290526
45792CB00008B/2275